SNEAKY PRESS

©Copyright 2023
Pauline Malkoun

The right of Pauline Malkoun to be identified as author of this work has been asserted by them in accordance with Copyright, Designs and Patents Act 1988.

All Rights Reserved.

No reproduction, copy or transmission of this publication may be made without written permission.
No paragraph of this publication may be reproduced, copied or transmitted save with the written permission of the publisher, or in accordance with the provisions of the Copyright Act 1956 (as amended).

Any person who commits any unauthorized act in relation to this publication may be liable to criminal prosecution and civil claims for damages.

A catalogue record for this work is available from the National Library of Australia.

ISBN 9781922641786

Sneaky Press is the imprint of Sneaky Universe.
www.sneakyuniverse.com
First published in 2023

Sneaky Press
Melbourne, Australia.

The Book of Random Airplane Facts

Sneaky Press

Contents

Random Facts about Airplane History	p.6
Types of Airplanes	p.8
Random Facts about Airports	p.10
Airplane Firsts	p.14
Airplane Records	p.16
Random Airplane Facts	p.18
More Random Airplane Facts	p.20
Airplane Idioms	p.24
Airplane Jokes	p.28
Random Facts about Paper Planes	p.32
Paper Plane Instructions	p.34

Random Facts about Airplane History

The Wright brothers, Wilbur and Orville were the first to fly an engine powered airplane on December 17, 1903.

They made four short flights at Kitty Hawk, North Carolina with Orville Wright as pilot.

Their plane was called the 1903 Wright Flyer.

You can see their plane on display in the National Air and Space Museum in Washington D.C.

French woman, Bessie Coleman is widely considered to be the first female pilot. She obtained her pilot's license in France in 1921. She became a renowned stunt pilot.

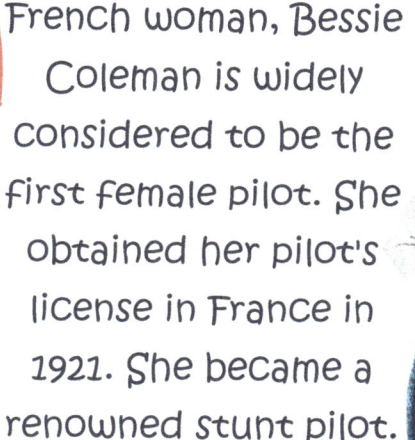

The engine, built by Charlie Taylor (an employee of the Wright brothers' employee) had 12 horsepower and was powered by petrol.

The first woman to fly solo across the Atlantic Ocean was Amelia Earhart, in May 1932.

Types of Airplanes

Airliners transport large numbers of people over long distances. These include the Airbuses and Boeing planes used by airlines.

The Turboprop is a propeller plane which can fly between 965 to 1609 km on a single flight.

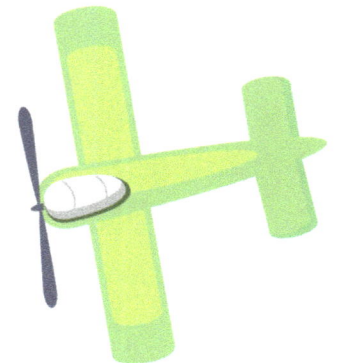

The Piston is a small plane which can fly between 482 to 643km per flight.

Jets usually fly at 980 km per hour and can reach heights of almost 15000m.

Bombers are military aircraft designed to carry and drop bombs on enemy targets – they are bigger and slower than fighter jets.

Fighter jets are military aircraft designed for combat against other aircraft.

Random Facts about Airports

With a runway just shy of 400m, the world's smallest airport is in the town of Juancho E. Yrausquin on the Dutch Caribbean island of Saba. Only small planes can land there.

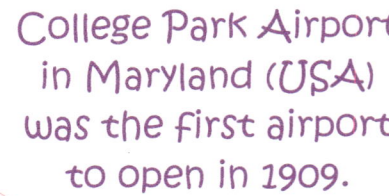

College Park Airport in Maryland (USA) was the first airport to open in 1909.

Bangkok's Suvarnabhumi Airport is home to the tallest control tower in the world, standing at a little over 131m tall.

In terms of land area, the largest airport in the world with 780 sq km is King Fahd International Airport in Saudi Arabia.

The airport with the most runways is Hartsfield-Jackson Atlanta International Airport in the United States, which has five parallel runways and two crossing runways.

The airport with the most passenger traffic in the world is Beijing Capital International Airport in China. Over 100 million passengers visited in 2019.

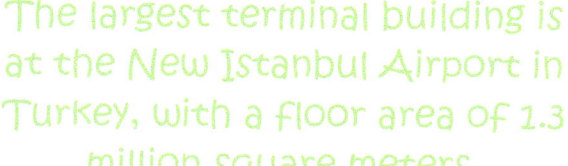

The largest terminal building is at the New Istanbul Airport in Turkey, with a floor area of 1.3 million square meters.

The longest runway in the world is 5500 metres long. It is at Qamdo Bamda Airport in Tibet.

Hamad International Airport in Qatar has a swimming pool.

Incheon International Airport in South Korea has an Indoor Garden.

Munich International Airport in Germany has an ice rink.

Vancouver International Airport in Canada has an Aquarium.

Kuala Lumpur International Airport in Malaysia has a Jungle boardwalk.

Hong Kong International Airport in Hong Kong has an Aviation Museum.

Airplane Firsts

In 1947, Chuck Yeager piloted Bell X-1, the first airplane to fly faster than the speed of sound, 343m per second.

The first flight which crossed the Atlantic ocean occurred in 1919 by the US Navy. The journey took 24 days.

In 1927, Charles Lindbergh became the first person to fly across the Atlantic on a solo, nonstop trip. It took him less than 34 hours.

The first transpacific flight from California, USA to Brisbane, Australia was piloted by Australian aviator Charles Kingsford Smith in 1928.

The first solar-powered flight around the world took over a year to complete. It started in March 2015 and finished in July 2016.

The first commercial airliner, The de Havilland Comet, made it's first flight for British Overseas Airways Corporation in 1952.

In 1939, German engineer Hans von Ohain flew the first jet-powered aircraft.

In 1986, the first non-stop flight around the world without refuelling took 9 days, 3 minutes and 44 seconds.

Airplane Records

The world's smallest plane weighs 162kg and has a wingspan of only 4.4m. It zooms through the air at speeds of up to 482km/h.

The longest nonstop flight record is held by Singapore Airlines. The flight travels over 15000km from Singapore to New Jersey in the United Sates. The flight is just over 18 hours long.

At 640000 kg, the Antanov AN_225 is the heaviest plane in the world.

18,288 metres is the highest a commercial airliner has ever flown. It was a Concorde airplane.

The highest a military airplane has flown is about 27,430 metres.

The largest passenger plane is the Airbus A380. It can carry up to 850 people.

Unveiled in February 2018, The Stratolaunch has the longest wingspan on a plane at 117 metres from tip to tip.

Reaching a speed of 3,530 kilometres per hour, the fastest plane ever was the Lockheed SR-71 Blackbird.

Wednesday 24 July 2019 was the busiest day in aviation ever recorded with over 225000 flights on that day.

Random Airplane Facts

Some planes can fly for up to 5 hours with only one of their engines working.

Black boxes are actually bright orange.

The Boeing 747's wingspan is longer than the Wright brothers' first flight distance.

The Concorde could fly at almost twice the speed of sound at 605 metre per second.

A Boeing 747 tank can hold over 220000 litres of fuel.

All pilots who fly internationally must speak at least a little English.

Airplane bathrooms can be unlocked from the inside and outside.

There are over 225km of wiring inside a Boeing 747.

More Random Airplane Facts

On any flight, the pilot and the co-pilot eat different meals.

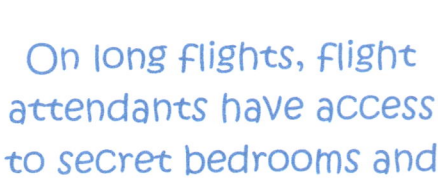

On long flights, flight attendants have access to secret bedrooms and bathrooms.

The humidity level in an airplane, usually set to 20%, is drier than the Sahara Desert, which has about 25% humidity.

The first meals served on a flight were sandwiches and a piece of fruit on a flight from London to Paris in 1919.

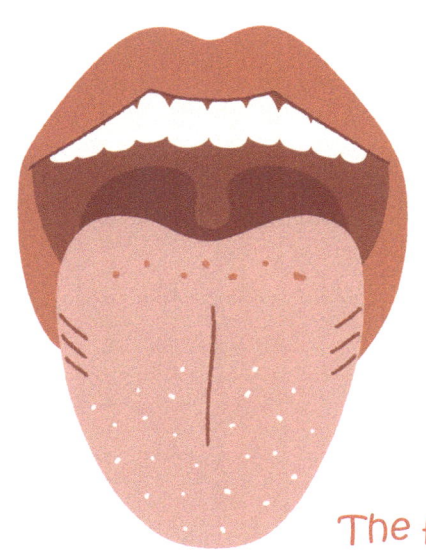

The sensitivity of tastebuds are reduced by 30% for salty and sweet foods during flight.

Established in 1919, Dutch carrier KLM is the world's oldest airline.

The first in-flight movie "The Lost World" was shown on a flight from London to Paris in 1925.

Commercial passenger jets usually cruise at an average speed between 740 to 925 km per hour.

Business Class was invented by Qantas in 1979.

Approximately one in six people suffer from aviophobia — the fear of flying.

A flight from London to Singapore takes about 12 hours. In 1934, it would have taken eight days and included 22 stopovers.

The Boeing 747 has approximately six million parts.

Leonardo da Vinci was fascinated with flight and designed several flying machines inspired by birds wings.

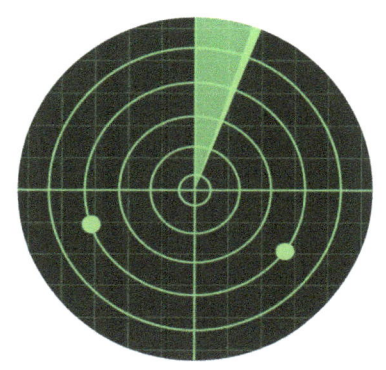

In addition to cars, SAAB make military planes, air traffic control systems and radar.

Rolls-Royce make plane engines as well as luxury cars.

Airplane Idioms

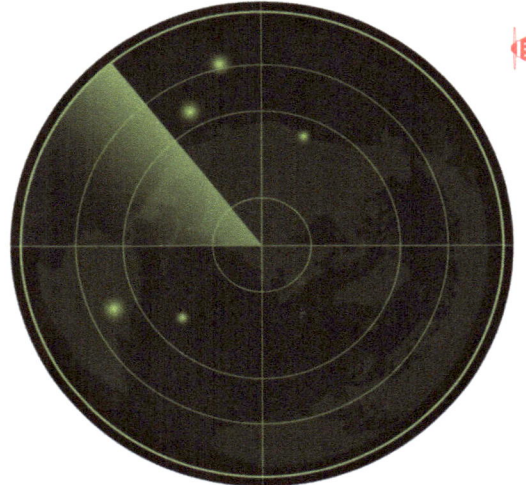

To fly into a rage means to lose control of one's temper and become very angry.

To fly under the radar means to go unnoticed.

To fly by the seat of one's pants means to improvise rather than following a set plan.

To fly blind means to move forward by guesswork.

To be flying high means to be very successful.

To cool one's jets means to calm down.

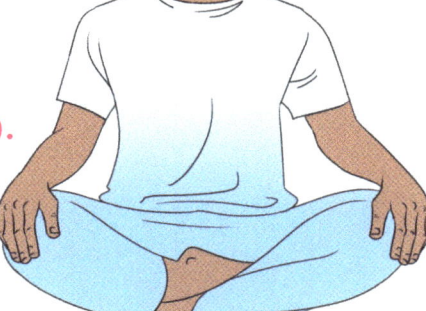

To be on a wing and a prayer means to rely on hope during a difficult situation.

To take someone under your wing means to look after and teach them.

To be in full flight means to be fleeing at great speed.

To take off means to become very successful.

If you are in a holding pattern it means you are in a state of waiting or uncertainty.

If there is turbulence ahead it means that their may be challenges or difficult times in the near future.

Airplane Jokes

Do you think invisible airplanes will ever be a thing?

I just don't see them taking off.

What flies, has a nose but can't smell?

An airplane!

A man called a travel agent and asked, "How long does it take to fly from London to New York?"

The agent said, "Just a minute…"

"Thank you," the man said and hung up.

During my flight the other day I asked the attendant to change my seat because of the crying baby next to me.

It turns out you can't change seats if the baby is yours.

What is it called when someone is sick of being in the airport?

Terminal illness.

What do you get when you cross an airplane with a magician?

A flying sorcerer.

Why did the student study in the airplane?

Because they wanted higher grades.

Two planes were chatting. One said, "Where should we go on vacation?"

The other replied: "I don't know. Let's wing it!"

What do you get if you cross a plane and a snake?

A Boeing Constrictor.

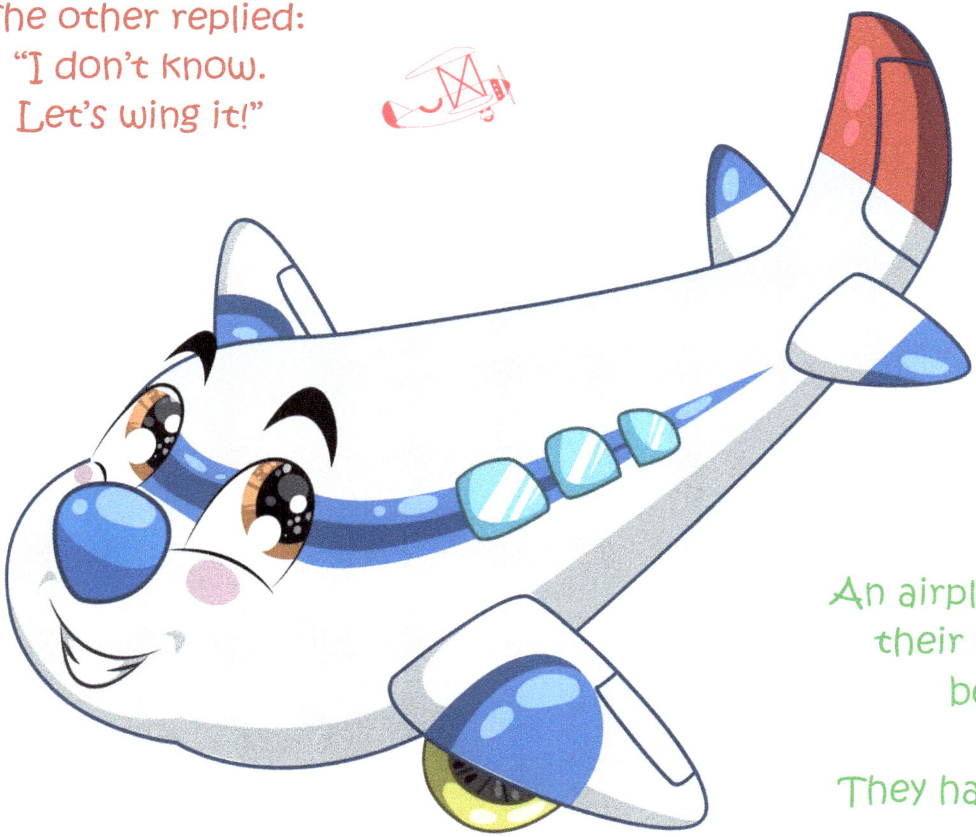

An airplane was sent to their room for bad behaviour.

They had bad altitude.

Paper Plane Facts

It is thought that paper planes originated in China 2000 years ago.

Record of the first modern paper planes go back to 1909.

The record for the longest paper plane flight is 29.2 seconds.

Students in Germany created the largest paper plane in September 2013. It had a wingspan of 18.2 meters.

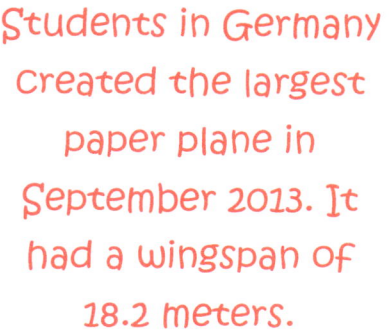

The longest distance a paper plane has glided through the air is just over 88 metres.

Make a Paper Plane in 5 Steps

1. Fold the paper in half.

3. Fold the top edges to the centre.

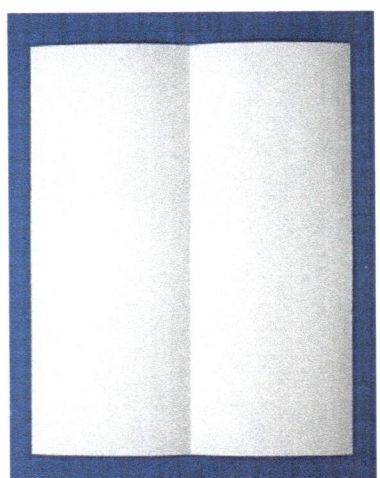

2. Unfold and then fold the corners into the centre line.

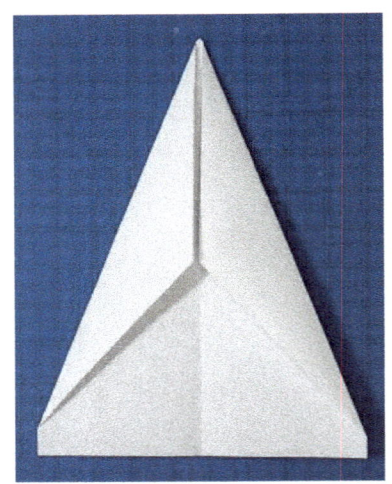

4. Fold the plane in half.

5. Fold the wings down to meet the bottom edge of the planes body.

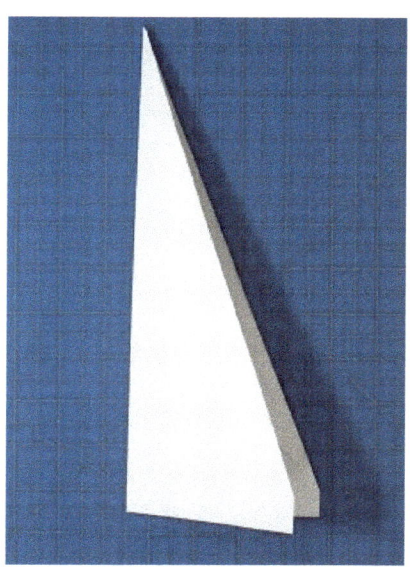

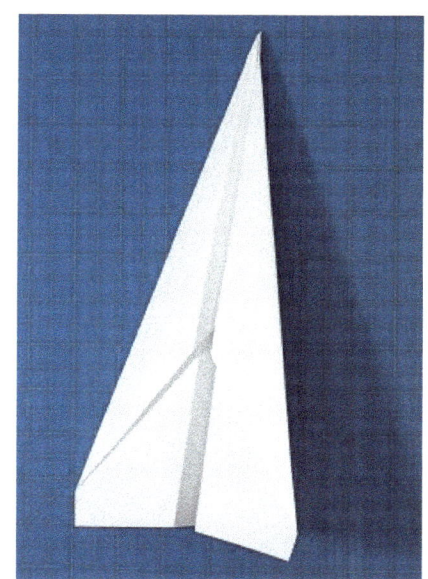

Thanks to FoldNfly.com for these instructions and images – for more planes check out https://www.foldnfly.com/#/1-1-1-1-1-1-1-1-2

Other titles in the Random Facts Series

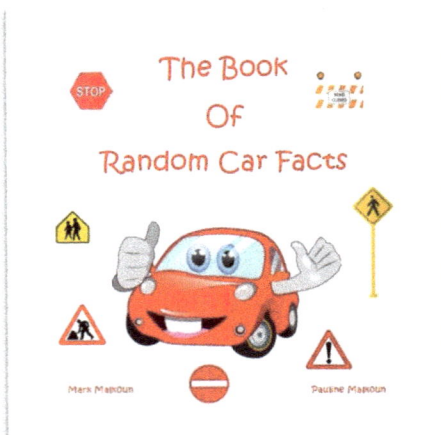
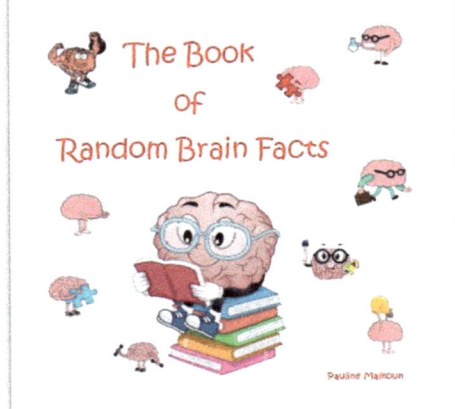
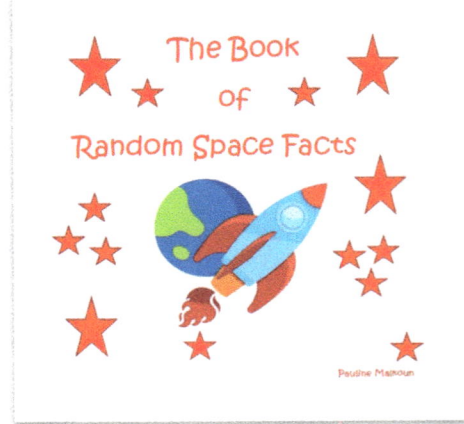
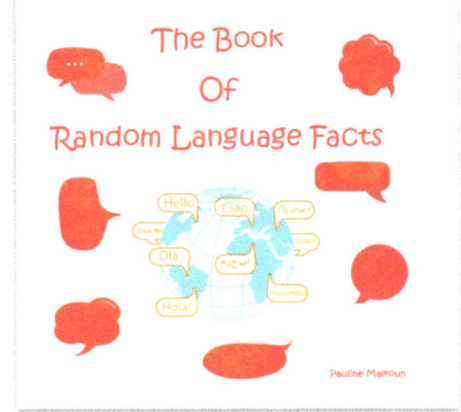

www.ingramcontent.com/pod-product-compliance
Lightning Source LLC
Chambersburg PA
CBHW051321110526
44590CB00031B/4426